is wet boy went dripping home.

This bad boy — this is true —
Put trick teeth in father's stew!

GNNG!

Gnick-gnack, Paddy wack
Gnasher wants a bone.

SPLAT

Lots of cake and stuff got thrown!

This bad boy cursed and swore,
Asked to push Dad's garden mower.

DAD'S BEE HIVE

This bad boy out did drive,
All the bees from father's hive.

GNOSHO

Gnick-gnack, Paddy wack
Gnasher wants a bone.

BUZZ

BUZZ

BUZZ

Funny buzzing on the phone?

Turn to inside back
page for more gnick-gnacks—

£3.85

CASTLE HASSLE

THE SOFTY SAVER

IT'S ALL RIGHT! YOU CAN COME OUT — DENNIS HAS GONE SWIMMING!

EH?

SOFTY SAVER SERVICE

PULL

THE POSTIE'S TROUSER REPAIR SHOP

PESKY GNASHER! HE BIT MY TROUSERS AGAIN!

ME TOO!

AND ME!

REPAIRS WHILE U WAIT

THE FAKE DAD MAKER

GET YOUR FAKE DAD HERE

SOLD

YOUR DENNIS IS A PEST!

WHAP

SEND HIM AWAY!

PUNISH HIM!

KICK

STOMP

SAVES ME A LOT OF TROUBLE!

Business

A LOT OF PEOPLE IN BEANOTOWN ARE KEPT IN WORK BECAUSE OF GNASHER AND ME . . .

THE CATAPULT AND REASHOOTER SHOP

WHAT A CUSTOMER!

TUM-TE-TUM!

PEAS

THE EMERGENCY MOBILE PSYCHIATRIST

CALM DOWN! MAYBE DENNIS WILL BE OFF SCHOOL TODAY!

TREMBLE

SHAKE

SCH

THE VERY STRONG DOG CLIPPER

NNG! HARD WORK, THIS!

OO—HA-HA-HA! WHAT A GAME! HO-HO-HO!

"IT'S A KNOCKABOUT" IS GREAT FUN! LET'S CHALLENGE THE SOFTIES TO A COMPETITION!

So—

YOU SOFTIES HAVE TO WALK ALONG THE PLANK WITH A BUCKET OF WATER BALANCED ON YOUR HEADS, WHILE WE TRY TO MAKE YOU SPILL IT!

SOUNDS JOLLY FUN!

So—

OUR BALLET TRAINING GIVES US PERFECT BALANCE!

PRANCE

BIG HAIRY SPIDERS!

FIERCE MICE!

CREEPIE CRAWLIES!

SPILL

SPILL

SHAKE

TREMBLE

SHUDDER

SHRIEK! DON'T SAY THOSE WORDS!

And—

PATHETIC! WE'LL BEAT THAT EASILY!

But—

ROGER THE DODGER!

THE BASH STREET KIDS!

BILLY WHIZZ!

HAW-HAW!

HO-HO!

TEE-HEE! THEY ALWAYS LAUGH LIKE THAT AT THE "BEANO" CHARACTERS! WE WIN!

HA! HA!

NOW FOR THE "ROLLING THE BARREL" RACE!

THIS WEEK'S COPY OF "THE BEANO"! QUICK, LADS!

FLATTEN
OI! WATCH WHERE YOU'RE GOING!

And—
WATCH, CHAPPIES! WE'RE PRETTY HIGH UP!
LET'S SEE YOU GO FASTER!

GNASH!

GNASH!
SCREAM! THAT HORRID DOG'S AFTER US!

SQUEAL! WE CAN'T STOP!
GASP! THEY'VE BEATEN US AGAIN!
ZOOM!

SPLINTER!
CRASH!
PHEW! WE'VE LANDED IN A NICE, SOFT SAND-PIT!

WE WON! WE WON!
BEATEN BY THE SOFTIES— WHAT A DISGRACE!

DENNIS, I WANT YOU TO WATER AND ROLL THE LAWN AND CHOP SOME STICKS!

GASP! YOU'VE DONE IT! IT'S THE SLIPPER FOR YOU!
BUT, DAD— WE'VE HELPED YOU FOR A CHANGE!

Dad returns from the house—
YES, BUT LOOK WHAT'S IN THE SLIPPER!
YAHOO!

IF YOU ARE SOMEWHERE YOU DON'T WANT TO BE, HERE'S MY GUIDE TO GETTING

THROWN OUT!

1. AT A BORING FILM . . .

. . . GET WALTER TO DO HIS FAMOUS VIKING SHADOW SHOW.

4. AT A CRICKET MATCH . . .

. . . SHOW YOUR HOLIDAY SLIDES ON THE SIGHT SCREENS.

SLIDES

5. IN THE MUSEUM . . .

. . . TRY SOME JOUSTING.

BEDTIME STORY

TIME TO TIDY UP THESE OLD ROSE-PETALS!

And—

THERE! THAT'S BETTER!

COMPOST HEAP →

ERK! IT'S RASHER!

POO! WHAT'S THAT HORRID SWEET SMELL?

DENNIS'S PET PIG

YOU CAN'T "STY" THERE—I'LL FIND YOU A NEW BED!

THERE'S A BED FOR YOU—A RIVER BED!

GREAT!

SPLUTCH!

RASHER LOVES SMELLY MUD!

But, upstream—

RIGHT, FRED, OPEN THE SLUICE-GATES!

SWOOSH!

OINK!

SWOOSH!

In a posh Chinese restaurant—

I'LL HAVE A VERY, VERY, VERY, VERY MILD CURRY ON A NICE BED OF RICE.

WALTER THE SOFTY

In the kitchen—

MM! SUPER BED OF RICE THIS!

GUZZLE!

RICE

GET OUT, FIENDISH CREATURE!

HMM! HAVE TO FIND ANOTHER BED FOR RASHER!

Soon—

WHERE CAN YOU SLEEP, PORKER PAL?

BEDDING FACTORY

ANOTHER REJECT FOR THE DUMP!

THAT'S IT, GNASHER. GOOD DOG!

BEDDING FACTORY

POINT

WATER BED

DUMP

SUCK

AHA! THAT DITCH CLEANER GIVES ME AN IDEA!

WATER BED

Soon—

SLURP!

BAH— CAVIARE AGAIN!

THIS SHOULD DO IT!

BLOW SUCK

RIGHT, GNASHER!

WATER BED

LIKE YOUR MUD BED, RASHER?

AH, BLISS!

Little known facts about...
SCHOOL

THE WHOLE SCHOOL STAFF WILL FIT INTO THE CUPBOARD IN DENNIS'S CLASSROOM!

PUSH!

THERE ARE 87 DIFFERENT COLOURS OF PAINT IN THE SCHOOL!

SPLAT!

SQUIRT!

ONLY 52 WILL WASH OUT!

SCRUB!

Later—
WOW! I DON'T BELIEVE IT!

OK, WALTER—IF IT'S A FIGHT YOU'RE AFTER...

FIGHTING?.. DON'T BE RIDICULOUS!

I'M HAVING A TEDDY TEA PARTY! THESE GLOVES ARE FOR SAFETY IN CASE I SPILL SOME LUKEWARM TEA ON MY DELICATE HANDIES!

Soon— EXCELLENT—I SEE YOU'RE BEING SAFETY CONSCIOUS!
THIS RUBBER SUCKER'S NOT FOR SAFETY!

GOT IT!

I'LL HAVE A STROLL ROUND THE GARDEN BEFORE TEA.
ALRIGHT, DEAR.

NOW TO GET THAT APPLE—ERK! DAD! WHERE DID YOU COME FROM?
YOW! MY NOSE!
P-Y-O-N-N-N-G!

SURELY YOU WOULDN'T FIRE AN ARROW WITHOUT SOMETHING ON THE TIP!
THROB THROB

OF COURSE NOT!

HAR-HAR! THAT TIP WASN'T VERY SAFE FOR DENNIS!
TWANG!
WHAP!

HAVING A BALL

SOFTY ACTION SQUAD!

But—

SOFTY
SPORTS
TODAY

THIS SHOULD BE A LAUGH!

So, inside—

FIRST EVENT—PUTTING THE SHOT!

GASP! THAT'S PRETTY TOUGH FOR YOU WEEDS!

SOFTIES

WE DON'T USE A REAL SHOT— WE COULDN'T LIFT IT! THIS IS MADE OF COTTON-WOOL!

NNNN!

OOOH— HOW STRONG!

GOOD SHOOTING, GNASHER!

SPLOOSH!

YOU HORRID ROTTERS!

SPLOT!

PRESENTATION SENSATION

ABOUT THIS TIME OF YEAR WE PRESENT OUR "MENACE OF THE YEAR" AWARD!

ABOUT THIS TIME OF YEAR WE PRESENT OUR "SOFTY OF THE YEAR" AWARD!

SOFTY OF THE YEAR

GNASHER DID SOME MENACING IN THE SUMMER...

CUT THE HEDGE FOR ME, GNASHER.

CHOMP! GNASH!

DAD WON'T TRY THAT AGAIN TEE-HEE!

DAD IS A LAZY BLOB

SHRIEK!

GOING INTO BAT, SPOTTY?

OH, NO...

SPOTTY WAS VERY SOFT AT ONE CRICKET MATCH!

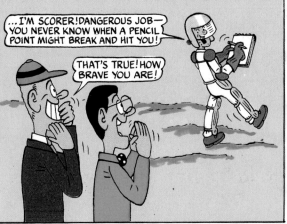

...I'M SCORER! DANGEROUS JOB— YOU NEVER KNOW WHEN A PENCIL POINT MIGHT BREAK AND HIT YOU!

THAT'S TRUE! HOW BRAVE YOU ARE!

REMEMBER WHEN DENNIS CHANGED ROUND A DIRECTION POST?...

And—

GREAT PIECE OF MENACING, THAT!

GROWL! SNARL!

SQUEAL!

I RECALL WHEN WALTER HAD TO SLEEP ON THE FLOOR...

...BECAUSE HIS BED WAS SO FULL OF TEDDIES AND CUDDLY TOYS!

PIE-FACE DID SOME BRILLIANT MENACING TO THE BRASS BAND!

HEH-HEH!

PIES

PIE

SILENCE

WHAT ABOUT WHEN BERTIE SPENT ALL HIS MONEY ON A CRASH-HELMET TO PROTECT HIM FROM NASTY, HEAVY SNOWFLAKES?

EEK!

WAH!

ERK!

DO YOU REMEMBER WHEN CURLY PUT ITCHING POWDER IN THE SOFTIES' DANCING PUMPS?

I'M THE MOST MENACING!

AND I'M THE SOFTEST!

I'LL WIN!

SO WILL I!

DENNIS! WHAT'S ALL THE NOISE ABOUT?

DAD'S VOICE
OO-ER! TIME WE WERE OFF!

IT'S BAD ENOUGH HAVING TO MODEL FOR MUM'S NEW DRESS WITHOUT ALL THIS NOISE!

HE FRIGHTENED DENNIS AWAY!

ER-FOR ME?

SOFTEST OUTFIT I'VE EVER SEEN!

GREEN SCENE

TIME

For this, menacing game you'll need tiddlywinks or buttons. Put your Dennis Book on the floor open at this page and try to feed Gnasher and Gnipper by landing counters in their mouths. Each player's turn consists of three shots with the first to score 50 points the winner. Score the highest number that the counter touches. Fire from one Softy Width away (about 1.5 very soft metres). Happy tiddling!

LOSE 5pts IF YOU LAND IN WALTER'S PRETTY BUTTON BOX.

10 pts

2 pts FOR A NEAR MISS

Soon—

BETTER TAKE ANOTHER DETOUR!

LET ME AT THEM!

SUPERB PIE COMPANY

Later—

PHEW! WE MUST HAVE BEEN WALKING FOR MILES. LET'S FIND A SEAT SOMEWHERE.

AT LEAST WE'VE KEPT PIE-FACE AWAY FROM ANY PIES!

WHAT'S THAT PLEASANT SOUND I HEAR?

DING-DONG!

OH, NO! IT CAN'T BE!

AFTER ALL WE'VE DONE TO KEEP PIE-FACE AWAY FROM PIES...

BILL'S GIANT PIES

... THE PIES COME TO PIE-FACE!

Just in time—

CLANG!

WELL DONE, GNASHER!

READER'S VOICE

At the fair—

"NAME THAT PIE" COMPETITION PRIZES GALORE

I DON'T SUPPOSE PICTURES OF PIES CAN DO MUCH HARM!

I MUST TRY THIS!

PORK—APPLE—CHICKEN —SHEPHERD'S—BILBERRY —MUD—MINCE—STEAK AND KIDNEY—HAM AND SEMOLINA—BLACKBIRD!

HERE'S YOUR PRIZE! WELL DONE, SON!

ASSORTED PIES

HE'S DONE IT AGAIN!

HEY! THOSE PIES ARE MINE!

CHOMP! GUZZLE! WE MUST FINISH THESE BEFORE PIE-FACE GETS FREE! CHEW! CHOMP!

CHOMP! SLURP!

Next day—

HEY! WHY SO SAD, PIE-FACE?

READER'S VOICE

BECAUSE I'M ALL ALONE TODAY!

TUT-TUT! VERY BAD CASES ALL OF YOU!

YOU CAN GUESS WHAT THEY'VE GOT, CAN'T YOU, READERS?

THE BOY'S GOT BOTTLE

HMM! I DON'T HAVE ANY BOTTLES TO PUT MY HOME-MADE LEMONADE IN.

FIZZ!

LEMONADE-MAKING KIT

I HAVEN'T ANY MONEY AS USUAL!

I'LL GIVE YOU 50p IF YOU FIND ME SOME BOTTLES!

FIZZ!

So—

AAA! A BABY'S BOTTLE!

SUCK

But—

PUSH OFF!

"BABY-FACE" FINLAYSON

SQUIRT!

SWOOSH!

In a chip shop—

LIKE SOME SAUCE ON YOUR CHIPS?

HEH-HEH! THAT'S ONE BOTTLE FOR ME!

WAH!

BLOOP!

UGH! WHAT A DISGUSTING MESS!

DISGUSTING MESS? LET ME AT IT!

SUCK

RASHER—GREEDY PIG

STONE CROWS

DID I EVER TELL YOU ABOUT THE TIME A SHORT-SIGHTED MOTHER CROW THOUGHT I WAS ONE OF HER BROOD..?

POOR CHILD! FELL OUT OF OUR NEST, DID YOU?

GNEEK!

HUH! NO CHANCE OF GETTING ANY BONES UP HERE!

Soon—

YEUCH! I'M GOING TO SNEAK AWAY AND CALL FOR HELP!

GASP! THIS IS TRICKY! FAIRLY TAKES YOUR BREATH AWAY!

But then—

PANT! I'LL HIDE IN HERE—GASP!—TILL I RECOVER—THEN I'LL GIVE DENNIS'S DAD A YELL!

And—

LET'S INSULT GNASHER! HE'LL BE IN HIS KENNEL—AND WE'RE SAFE UP HERE!

GNASHER'S A SOFTY DOG!

BOO TO YOU, SOFTY GNASHER!

TEE-HEE! I'M ENJOYING THIS!

YES—GOOD JOB GNASHER CAN'T CLIMB TREES!

GNASH!

YIKES!

BUT...EEK!

GNASH! GNASH!

EH?

WHAT?

HOW'D HE GET UP HERE?

HOW'D HE GET UP HERE?

MAYBE A LITTLE BIRD WILL TELL THEM! GNEE! GNEE!

Dennsil and Gnashtel

(A MENACING FAIRY STORY)

Once upon a time there were two children, Dennsil and Gnashtel. Their mother didn't like them very much. Dennsil she didn't like because he was always in trouble. Gnashtel she didn't like because he was covered in black hair and always bit the postman. This was quite natural as he was a dog but she was pretty dense and hadn't realised this.

Anyway, she didn't like them, so she sent them out to walk in the woods hoping they would get lost or perhaps eaten by a very large hamster (see — told you she was thick).

FOOD SHOP

The woods were pretty thick too and soon Dennsil and Gnasthel WERE lost. They wandered about for hours getting more and more hungry. There were plenty of fruit trees and even some food shops in the woods but since Dennsil only ever ate sweets and Gnashtel preferred posties' trousers, this was not a lot of help to them.

The wood they were in was a strange place with some very odd buildings in it. King Tredbert the Trampolinist had his bouncy castle there. This was far bigger than those things you see at fairgrounds these days. This one was big enough to hold seven Queens, 52 Princes and Princesses, 104 Dukes, 207 Lords and two overworked servants, every one of them sea sick from Tredbert's non stop trampolining. There was also a library made entirely of books, from which you could borrow real bricks. The sauna bath made from butter had unfortunately melted by the time Dennsil and Gnashtel arrived.

BOUNCE!

SAUNA

Dennsil and Gnashtel wer delighted. They tried the knocker to se if anyone was at home. The knocker wa made of marshmallow and made n sound at all as it knocked against th peanut brittle door. No one answere (you will be surprised to hear) so the did what people always do when no on answers a door — they began to eat th house.

FLUMP! FLUMP!

GNASH! RIP!

GNOW!

OW! OW! OW!

Soon, though, they came to one of the oddest buildings in the wood. It was a house made out of sweets and posties' trousers. The walls were chocolate pebble dashed with mint humbugs, the slates on the roof were crisps, the liquorice chimney puffed out candyfloss smoke and round the doors were pillars of posties' trousers.

They chomped away merrily until they could eat no more. The house was hardly touched. A house will feed two boys (even if one is a dog) for a long long time. Eating too much of it at once will only give you a sore stomach. Dennsil and Gnashtel had found this out and lay groaning on the ground. "Ow! Ow! Ow!" said Dennsil. "Gnow! Gnow! Gnow!" said Gnashtel who spoke in a very odd way.

This groaning was far louder than the sound of the marshmallow door knocker. So loud that it woke up the owner of the house who had been fast asleep inside all along. He came outside to see what was going on. He was not at all pleased when he found out. He jumped up and down shouting at Dennsil and Gnashtel — just like you would do if you found someone eating your house. The next thing you would do is call the police but in fairy tales things are done differently. The man in the house decided the best way to punish them was to put them in the oven and bake them into a pie. Very odd!

He didn't think so, though, and in no time Dennsil and Gnashtel were inside his oven.

The man turned the fruit drop knob to turn the chocolate oven on and sat back to wait for his pie to cook.

It is one thing to build a house of sweets and posties' trousers, but making an oven out of chocolate is just silly. Almost as soon as it was switched on it melted. Dennsil and Gnashtel were covered in soft chocolate and emerged from the wreck of the oven looking like a pair of very nasty space aliens from the planet Chocco. The owner of the house took one look at them and ran screaming into the woods roaring "Help! I'm being pursued by two space aliens from the planet Chocco!"

Many weird things went on in this wood but no one was going to believe that kind of rubbish, so the man was soon locked up in a home for liars who told particularly large whoppers, where he stayed for the rest of his life.

But what of Dennsil and Gnashtel?

Once they had licked the chocolate off, Dennsil and Gnashtel lived happily ever after in the house made of sweets until one day they ate through the foundations and the whole lot collapsed on them.

'MARBLE'OUS STUFF

I COULD USE THESE BEADS.

I'LL LEND YOU MONTY HERE...

SHRIEK!

SNAP!

...IF YOU LEND ME YOUR BEADS! THANKS!

Shortly—

HOW FASCINATING!

CLICK! CLICK! CLICK!

Then—

ERK!

SNIP!

THEY'LL MAKE SUPER MARBLES!

BETTER HURRY OR I'LL BE LATE FOR THE CONTEST!

TOY SHOP

GAMES

MARBLES MARBL

I'VE BOUGHT DENNIS MARBLES. I'LL GET NO PEACE OTHERWISE!

MARBLES

GA!

CRUNCH!

OO! OW! OUCH! YOW!

MARBLES

GNEEK!

I'M UNFIT FOR THE MARBLE CHAMPIONSHIPS! GROAN! WHAT A WAY TO LOSE YOUR TITLE!

HMM! I ENJOYED A GAME OF MARBLES IN MY YOUTH!

MENACE MARBLE CHAMPIONSHIP

I'LL TAKE DENNIS'S PLACE!

DAD'S TROPHY CABINET

MENACE MARBLE

GOLDEN WHACK

SILVER THUMP

DAD KEPT THE TROPHY IN THE FAMILY, ANYWAY!

WHAT A LOAD OF RUBBISH

OH FOR THE WINGS OF A DOG!

SUPER! AREN'T BUTTERFLIES AMAZING? SUCH GRACE! SUCH BEAUTY!

FLUTTER

DENNIS'S DAD

SUCH SOPPINESS!

GNESH!

WALTER, PRINCE OF SOFTIES

DID YOU KNOW THAT IN SOUTH AMERICA THEY HAVE GIANT BUTTERFLIES?...

WISH HE'D SHUT UP ABOUT BUTTERFLIES — SOFT THINGS!

A-Z OF BUTTERFLIES

I KNOW HOW TO PUT WALTER OFF BUTTERFLIES!

LINEN CUPBOARD

THAT'S THE WAY, GNASHER!

SQUEEZE

Later, at Walter's house—

HEY, WALTER— ONE OF THOSE GIANT BUTTERFLIES MUST HAVE COME OVER TO BRITAIN AND LAID ITS EGGS!

WHAT MAKES YOU SAY THAT?

THAT MUST BE ONE OF ITS CATERPILLARS!

SQUEAL! A HORRID CREEPIE-CRAWLIE!

SLITHER

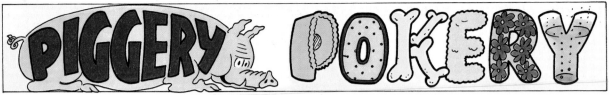

IN THE PARK —

LOVELY MUD!

OOPS! CAN'T STOP!

MY BACK'S KILLING ME, PICKING UP THIS LITTER!

YOUR PROBLEM'S SOLVED!

A HAM ROLL!

LITTER

THIS IS FOR YOUR PIG'S HELP!

COO! THANKS!

PICK

LITTER

WONDER IF THERE'S ANY MOULDY COMPOST IN WALTER'S GARDEN?

THUNDER!

LITTLE SOFT BOY

SQUIRT!

ERK!

OIL

BUMP!

OUT OF MY WAY!

OIL

SPLUDGE!

I'M FROM THE FAIRGROUND. CAN I HIRE YOUR PIG?

WHINE!

EH? SURE!

AND —

GREASY PIG

10p A RIDE

NOW I'VE GOT MONEY FOR MYSELF AND ENOUGH TO BUY YOU A SLAP-UP FEED!

OINK!

GNASH!

IN A POSH RESTAURANT —

I'LL READ OUT THE MENU — YOU GRUNT TO TELL ME WHAT YOU WANT!

LOVELY FLOWERS!

HOTEL POSH MENU

SCOTCH BROTH, MELON, STEAK PIE, SPAGHETTI, FISH AND CHIPS, CUSTARD, PRUNES RHUBARB TART —

HOTEL POSH MENU

GRUNT! GRUNT! GRUNT! GRUNT! GRUNT! GRUNT! GRUNT! GRUNT!

THAT GREEDY PIG'S EATING ALL THE FOOD TOGETHER! HOW DISGUSTING!

CHOMP!

GORGE!

BONES AND CHIPS

CRUNCH! GNASH!

MEDICINE MENACIN'

LIKE A NICE CHOP, DENNIS?

SLURP! YOU BET!

WELL, YOU CAN *CHOP* SOME STICKS — THIS IS A STEAK! HAR-HAR!

GRR! TRICKED!

LUCKY I'VE GOT GNASHER! WISH I COULD GET MY OWN BACK ON DAD!

BZZZZZ!

Later—

ERK!

SPLUDGE!

SERVES YOU RIGHT FOR PESTERING MY TURTLES!

TURTLE POOL

Back home—

SLOP! SLOP! SLOP!

YOUR FEET ARE SOAKING! YOU'LL CATCH A COLD...

...UNLESS YOU HAVE A MUSTARD FOOT BATH.

BAH! I HATE BEING DOCTORED UP!

MUSTARD POWDER

LITTLE SOFT CHAPPIE

CHESS SET

LOOK AT ALL THE TOYS WALTER GOT FOR PASSING HIS EXAMS.

ALL I GOT FOR **NOT** PASSING WAS A WHACKING FROM DAD!

HEAT FROM WHACKING

I KNOW—I'LL MAKE MY OWN TOYS!

HOW DO YOU LIKE MY PORTRAIT OF DEAR FLUFFY?

PURR-FECT!

I'D LIKE TO SHOW IT TO SOMEONE!

LOOK, GNASHER!

SNARL!

GNASH! GNASH! GNASH! GNASH!

GREAT JIGSAW PUZZLE, THIS!

Little known facts about...

GNASHER and GNIPPER

THE POSTIE WHO DELIVERS TO THEIR HOUSE HAS 102 UNIFORMS — ALL WITH THE LEGS GNASHED!

DAD'S GARDEN NOW CONTAINS MORE BONES THAN SOIL!

THE RECORD NUMBER OF CATS UP A TREE IS 243!

SOFTY BEFORE WICKET

GREAT! A COUPLE OF THOSE SOFTIES ARE OFF TO THE SEASIDE FOR THE DAY!

BYE-'BYE, CHUMMIES! BOO-HOO!

WALTER, SOFTEST OF ALL SOFTIES

BOO-HOO-HOO! SOB! SOB! SOB! I'VE NO-ONE TO PLAY WITH!

YOU'LL HAVE TO LET WALTER PLAY WITH YOU, OR WE'LL BE FLOODED OUT!

WE'RE GOING TO PLAY CRICKET. YOU FIELD, WALTER.

THUMP!

So—

THWACK!

MUST KEEP MY HANDIES SOFT.

HAND CREAM

CATCH IT! CATCH IT!

BAH! USELESS SOFTY!

SLIP

ERK!

Later... Walter's turn to bat—

WHIMPER! DON'T BOWL TOO HARD NOW!

TAP!

OOOH!

TOPPLE

OUT! HOW PATHETIC!

YOU BOWL!

HORRORS! NO! NO! I CAN'T DO THAT!

WHY NOT, FOR GOODNESS SAKE?

I COULDN'T FORGIVE MYSELF IF I CRUSHED ONE OF THOSE LOVELY DAISIES!

WHY NOT WORK THE SCOREBOARD?

SCOREBOARD

VERY WELL.

SCOREBOARD

IDIOT! YOU'RE MEANT TO KEEP THE SCORE— NOT DO SUMS!

YOU BE UMPIRE—HERE— KEEP MY JERSEY!

AND MINE!

HOWZAT?

ZZZ!

WAKEN UP!

HELP! WHAT? I WAS SO LOVELY AND COSY I FELL ASLEEP!

HOW DID YOU GET ON PLAYING WITH WALTER?

HIM? HE'S JUST A MENACE!

WALTER—A MENACE? GASP!

THE SHAME!

HEH-HEH!

I'VE BOUGHT MYSELF A DRINK...WONDER WHERE GNASHER IS, BY THE WAY?

TRIP

OOPS!

HUH! NOT A DROP LEFT— FOR ME, THAT IS!

SLURP!

AH! I'LL GET A DRINK HERE.

HUH! IT DOESN'T SEEM TO BE WORKING — BUT I CAN HEAR WATER GURGLING INSIDE.

GURGLE!

YEOW!

SPLOOSH!

GNEEK!

AW, GNASHER, YOU MIGHT HAVE LET ME GET A DRINK FIRST!

ANGRY GNASH!

AH, WELL, I'M HOME NOW. I'LL GET A DRINK HERE.

THE WATER'S OFF, DENNIS. THEY'RE DOING SOMETHING TO THE PIPES.

JUST MY LUCK!

THERE MIGHT STILL BE A CUP OF TEA LEFT IN THE POT.

AH! THAT'LL DO NICELY!

AT LAST I'LL GET RID OF MY THIRST!

WATCH THIS FAULTY HANDLE

NOW FOR A DRINK— ERK!

SMASH!

Then—

KNOCK! KNOCK!

WATER! I NEED WATER!

CRAWL

WHAT DO YOU WANT?

THOUGHT YOU MIGHT LIKE TO SEE THE LOVELY ANGEL FISH I'VE BOUGHT.

WALTER, THE LITTLE SOFT BOY

BAH! THAT FISH IS JUST A SOFTY LIKE YOU!

SOFTY? I AM NOT A SOFTY!

TAKE THAT!

SLURP! THAT'S BETTER! THANKS FOR COMING ROUND, WALTER!

Little known facts about... RASHER

RASHER KNOWS OVER 1000 TURNIP RECIPES!

TURNIP PIE
TURNIP JELLY
TURNIP OMELETTE
TURNIP CAKE
TURNIP CURRY

LIFTING RASHER REQUIRES A PORK LIFT TRUCK!

LIFT!

DAD'S TURNIP STORE HAS STEEL DOORS SIX INCHES THICK!

DAD'S TURNIP STORE

CRASH!

BRINGING HOME the BACON

MUST KEEP TRYING!

HEY! WHAT'S THAT THE SOFTIES ARE SHAKING OVER ONE ANOTHER?

GREAT! MAYBE IT'S PEPPER!

EEK!

HUH! IT'S NOT PEPPER...

SCREECH TO HALT

...IT'S PERFUMED TALCUM POWDER. I MIGHT HAVE KNOWN!

REEL

TEE-HEE! SERVES YOU RIGHT!

OH, BOTHER! MY CONTINENTAL QUILT'S BURST!

OH-OH!

IT—IT'S GOING TO WORK!

ATCHOO!

JUST IN TIME. MY NOSE HAS BEEN BLOCKED ALL MORNING — AND IT'S NOT NEARLY SO MUCH FUN COMING HOME FOR LUNCH IF YOU CAN'T SMELL WHAT MUM'S COOKING FOR YOU!

This bad boy, up to tricks,
Blocked up the front door with bricks.

Gnick-gnack, Paddy wack
Gnasher wants a bone.

Mum's quite happy o
own!

Used a ball he'd carved from stone.

This bad boy thinks its great,
Spotty Perkins to inflate.

Gnick-gnack, Paddy wack
Gnasher wants a bone.

Menace house engulfed by foam!

This bad boy runs off, then,